Walking Wi

Wisdom from Brother Lawrence

Patricia Mitchell, General Editor

the WORD
among us

The Word Among Us Press
9639 Doctor Perry Road
Ijamsville, Maryland 21754

Design by David Crosson
Copy Editor: Laura Worsham

Library of Congress Cataloging-in-Publication Data

Lawrence, of the Resurrection, Brother, 1611-1691.
    [Pratique de la présence de Dieu. English. Selections]
    Walking with the father : wisdom from Brother Lawrence :
selections from the Practice of the presence of God / by Brother
Lawrence of the Resurrection.
        p.   cm.
    ISBN 0-932085-21-0 (pbk. : alk. paper)
    1. Christian life—Catholic authors.   I. Title.
BX2349.L3825 1999
248.4'82—dc21
                                     98-50286
                                          CIP

Made and printed in the United States of America

Table of Contents

Introduction

Brother Lawrence of the Resurrection was a seventeenth-century lay Carmelite brother who took literally the words of St. Paul to "pray constantly" (1 Thessalonians 5:17). At every waking moment, Brother Lawrence praised his Father, thanked him, and remained in his presence. As he cultivated this habit, he found himself continually in God's presence, so much so that Lawrence sometimes felt he could hardly contain his joy.

"If I were a preacher, I would preach nothing else than the practice of the presence of God; and if I were a director of souls, I would recommend to everyone that they continually converse with God, because I believe it is so vital and even easy to practice," Brother Lawrence once wrote. From what we know about his life, he took every opportunity to tell others what he had discovered about living in God's presence, which he believed was for everyone—lay people and religious alike.

Christians for three centuries have treasured *The Practice of the Presence of God*—the collection of Brother Lawrence's letters and conversations in which he reveals the secrets of walking with God at all times. His advice is especially pertinent today, when the hectic pace of modern life often makes it difficult to spend quality time with the Lord. Prayer is the way we come to know God. If we can to any degree practice the presence of God as we perform our day-to-day duties, then we will know the Lord intimately and be filled with the same peace and joy that Brother Lawrence experienced.

To make Brother Lawrence's wisdom more accessible to readers, we have taken the original book and divided it by topic. Where the language would have sounded awkward to modern readers, we have revised sentence structures and words, all the while retaining their original meaning. Our goal was to produce a book that is easy to pick up and read at any time—all at once, or in small doses.

As you read *Wisdom from Brother Lawrence*, you will notice that some of the excerpts are in the first person, directly from Brother Lawrence, while others are paraphrases of his sayings. This is because the original book included letters he had written himself, and also recollections of conversations he had with his religious superior, which are in the superior's words. Each excerpt in this book identifies its source, whether from the letters, conversations, or "spiritual maxims," which are summaries of his teachings.

Brother Lawrence's message is, in some ways, simple, and he even repeats himself. However, his insights about faith, love, humility, and the need to surrender ourselves completely to the Lord are based on his own experience of a truly intimate union with God. It is our hope at *The Word Among Us* that this book will deepen your consciousness of the Holy Spirit's presence in your life. Throughout your day, may you find yourself silently praying and conversing with your Constant Companion, offering him continual praise and thanksgiving for his love and care.

The Word Among Us Press
Feast of the Presentation of the Lord
February 2, 1999

The Life of
Brother Lawrence

*"I turn my little omelette in the pan for the love of God;
when it is finished, if I have nothing to do, I prostrate myself
on the ground, and adore my God, who gave me the grace to
make it, after which I arise, more content than a king."*
— Brother Lawrence

Brother Lawrence of the Resurrection spent most of his life as a monk in a Carmelite monastery in Paris, and for much of that time, he worked in the kitchen. In this very ordinary setting, he discovered the presence of God as powerfully as if he had been on a spiritual retreat. Whatever he did, in every moment of the day, this humble man sought out the Lord—and found him. His success is our blessing, for 300 years after his death, his words can teach us how to live in the presence of God no matter how busy we are or how many responsibilities we face. Given our fast-paced lives, Brother Lawrence is like a modern prophet. He shows us how to incorporate our spirituality into our routine actions, and how to make our often disjointed lives into a seamless whole that is pleasing to the Lord.

While Brother Lawrence's ability to stay centered on the Lord was extraordinary, there was nothing out of the ordinary about him. The Lord delights in using the humblest men and women to experience his treasures, and this was the case with Brother Lawrence. He was born Nicholas Herman in Lorraine, France, probably in 1611. Much of what we know about his life is contained in a eulogy written by Abbé Joseph de Beaufort, who was the superior at the monastery. According to de Beaufort, Nicholas' mother and father were "upright people who led an exemplary life" and who "inspired in him the fear of God in his childhood."

Captured as a Spy

As a young man, Nicholas became a soldier, joining his fellow country men of Lorraine to fight in the Thirty Years War. He was captured by German troops as a spy, and they threatened to hang him. Abbé de Beaufort wrote that, instead of becoming frightened, Nicholas told his captors that he was not a spy, and that since his conscience was free of any crime, he did not worry about dying. The officers then released him, and he rejoined his command.

When Swedish troops made their way into Lorraine and attacked the town of Rambervilliers, Nicholas was wounded. His injury forced him to return to his parents' home, where he had time to think about his life. According to de Beaufort, "He reflected often upon the perils of his profession, the vanity and the corruption of the century, the instability of men, the treason of the enemy, and the infidelity of his friends." He decided to "give himself wholly to God and to repair his past conduct."

At some point during this time—Brother Lawrence said it was when he was eighteen—he experienced a life-changing grace. One day, while looking at a tree stripped of its leaves, he reflected that soon new leaves would appear with flowers and fruits in bloom. This reflection gave him a profound insight into the providence and power of God, and he fell completely in love with the Lord.

For a short time, Nicholas served as a footman to William de Fieubet, treasurer of the king of France. However, he described himself as "a clumsy lummox who broke everything." An uncle who was a Carmelite friar encouraged him to join a monastery, but he met a wealthy man who had given away his possessions to live the life of a hermit and—inspired by his example—he decided to adopt the same lifestyle.

Lay Brother in Paris

Nicholas quickly realized that this way of life was not for him—he was too young in the spiritual life to live without a community of other Christians and a rule of life to keep him on a steady course. Still, he was frightened by the idea of perpetual vows and, for a while, he procrastinated. Eventually, he went to Paris to apply for admission as a lay brother at the monastery of the Discalced Carmelites on Rue de Vaugirard, and was given the name Brother Lawrence of the Resurrection.

In the first ten years of his religious life, Lawrence experienced intense interior suffering, which he referred to briefly in his letters. Even as the Lord began to shower his graces on him, Lawrence felt radically unworthy of them. His sins were always before him and he began to wonder whether his experiences of God were an illusion. He also believed he would be damned. "His soul was plunged into such bitterness and such thick darkness that neither from heaven nor from earth did he receive any help," wrote de Beaufort, who added that "faith alone was his support."

Finally, Brother Lawrence abandoned himself completely to the Lord, resolving to endure this suffering "not only the rest of his life, but even for all eternity, if it so pleased God." From that moment, God opened his eyes and gave him a ray of light that ended his fears and pain. Confronted with the brilliance of God's glory on the one hand and his own sin on the other, Brother Lawrence said that he decided "to remain in the presence of God with all the humility of a useless but faithful servant."

Tranquility in the Kitchen

At first, Brother Lawrence found it difficult to stay continually in God's presence, but when he realized he had passed some time without remembering the Lord, he simply confessed his fault and took up the practice again. He found he could enjoy God's presence while at work as well as in prayer: "I possess God as tranquilly in the bustle of my kitchen—where sometimes several people are asking me different things at one time—as if I were on my knees before the Blessed Sacrament." He renounced everything but God, forgetting himself entirely and leaving everything—even his own virtue and salvation—in God's hands.

Beneath a "common exterior," said de Beaufort, Brother Lawrence shined with wisdom and began to teach his fellow monks all that he had learned while communicating with God. He "spoke freely and with extreme kindness," and his genial presence "gave confidence and made you feel immediately that you could reveal anything to him and that you had found a friend." His holiness soon became known beyond the monastery and others sought out his wisdom. One French bishop remarked that Brother Lawrence's pure love for God made him live on earth as if he were already a saint in heaven.

As Brother Lawrence mentions himself, he was lame in one leg for many years. Eventually, his leg developed an ulcer, and after many years in the kitchen, he was sent to a less physically demanding job in the shoe repair shop. He suffered through two severe illnesses with "the same serenity of soul that he had retained in the most vigorous health," said de Beaufort. During his third and last illness, he remained joyful and pleased that he could suffer for the love of God. He also was completely fearless about the prospect of dying. He told one brother, "I am doing what I will do for all eternity. I am blessing God, praising God, adoring him and loving him with all my heart. That is our whole profession, brothers, to adore God and to love him, without worrying about the rest." Brother Lawrence died on February 12, 1691, at the age of 80.

The Practice of the Presence of God

Although Brother Lawrence destroyed much of what he had written during his lifetime, Abbé de Beaufort was able to gather up what he could: sixteen letters, some recollections of his conversations with him, and the spiritual "maxims"—much of which were taken from the letters and conversations. Of the sixteen letters, thirteen were addressed to a nun, two to lay women, and one to a priest. This odd assortment eventually became known as *The Practice of the Presence of God*, a book that captures the essence of divine union with God and has remained a treasured spiritual classic through the centuries.

Abbé de Beaufort knew that Brother Lawrence's words would be beneficial to anyone who read them because his method of consciously abiding in God's presence "is not a theoretical devotion, nor one that can be practiced only in cloisters." Everyone, said de Beaufort, "is obliged to adore and to love God; and no one can perform these two great duties as he ought without establishing with God an interchange of love that gives us access to him at every moment, like children who can scarcely stand without their mother's help." Like little children, we need to be reminded often of God's great love for us and his desire to be with us always. Brother Lawrence can be our inspiration as we go through each day, practicing the presence of the Lord at every moment and in every situation.

1

A Silent Conversation

Practicing the presence of God is a conscious movement of our souls to God, recalling that God is present with us every moment. This experience can be made either by the imagination or by the intellect.

I know a person who for forty years has practiced an intellectual presence of God, to which he gives several other names. Sometimes he calls it a simple act, or a clear and distinct knowledge of God, sometimes an indistinct vision or loving look at God. Other times he terms it attention to God, silent conversation with God, confidence in God, the life and the peace of the soul. To sum it up, this friend told me that all these manners of the presence of God are but synonyms that signify one identical thing, which is now natural to him.

Spiritual Maxims

My friend says that by frequently recalling to his mind the presence of God, he has formed such a habit that, as soon as he is free of his normal duties and even often when he is engrossed in them, the tip of his spirit rises without any effort on his part and remains as suspended and fixed in God, above all things, as in its center and place of rest. Since in this rest he feels his soul almost always accompanied by faith, that satisfies him. That is what he calls the actual presence of God, which includes all the other kinds of presence and much more. Now he lives as if there were no one but God and himself in the world; everywhere he goes he converses with God, asks him for what he needs, and rejoices with him unceasingly in a thousand ways.

Spiritual Maxims

His chief concern has been to stay always with our heavenly Father and to do nothing, to say nothing, to think nothing, that can displease him—without any other intention than that of the Father's pure love. Just now he is so close to the Lord that he receives from the Spirit continual grace on all sorts of occasions. For about thirty years, his soul has enjoyed interior delights so constant and sometimes so great that, in order to contain them and prevent them from becoming apparent, he is forced to act childishly, in ways that seem more like folly than devotion.

First Letter

Brother Lawrence once told me that the foundation of his entire spiritual life had been an exalted understanding and esteem of God in faith. Once he understood this, he had no other concern. He would immediately reject every other thought, so that all his actions flowed out of his love for Jesus. If many hours passed without thinking of the Lord, he never got upset about it. Instead, he confessed his weakness to God and returned to him with even more confidence. As he looked back, he realized how unhappy he had been when he forgot the Lord.

Third Conversation

Brother insisted that we must form a habit of frequently thinking of the presence of God by conversing with him constantly. He felt that it was a shame when we stopped this conversation with the Lord to think of trivial things. If we nourish our souls with the grandeur of God, we will have great joy knowing that we belong to him.

First Conversation

In the beginning, Brother declared, a little effort was needed to form the habit of conversing continually with God and telling him all that he was doing. After some care, however, he would feel himself awakened by God's love, without any effort.

Second Conversation

Brother Lawrence said everything consisted in renouncing, once and for all, anything we recognize which does not lead to God. That way, we can get used to having a continual conversation with him, without any mystery and with great simplicity. We only have to recognize the Spirit, intimately present within us, and to address ourselves to the Lord at all times—to ask his help, to know his will when we are not sure, and to obey him when are sure of what he wants. We should offer these actions to our Father before doing them and thank him afterwards for having done them for his sake.

In this continual conversation, we would also be engaged in praising, adoring, and loving God unceasingly for his infinite goodness and perfection.

Fourth Conversation

According to Brother Lawrence, thoughts spoiled everything, and the evil began there. He said we must be careful to reject thoughts as soon as we realized that they were not necessary to whatever we were doing at the present moment or to our salvation. This made it possible to resume our conversation with God, in which we have peace.

Second Conversation

What indescribable joy and peace we experience, knowing the great treasure of God's presence continually in our hearts! We no longer anxiously struggle to find the Lord, and we do not need to worry any more about looking for the Holy Spirit, for we have discovered God's presence and are free to receive this treasure at any moment.

First Letter

The first way to acquiring the presence of God is great purity of life.

The second way is a great fidelity to the practice of this presence and to the interior gazing upon God in faith. This must always be done gently, humbly, and lovingly, without giving way to any trouble or anxiety.

Spiritual Maxims

You must take particular care that this interior glance, although it may last only a moment, precedes your usual duties, that from time to time it accompanies them, and that you finish all of them with it. Since time and much effort are needed to acquire this practice, one should not be discouraged when one fails, because a habit can be formed only with difficulty. Once it is formed, however, knowing God's presence will be easily attained and done with pleasure.

Spiritual Maxims

Those who are beginning to practice God's presence often say, interiorly, some phrase such as "My God I am all yours," "God of love, I love you with all my heart," "Lord, do with me according to your will," or some other words that love inspires at the time. But they must take care that their mind does not wander nor return to worldly concerns. They must attach their mind to God alone, so that, uniting their will to God's will, it may only dwell with God.

Spiritual Maxims

Drawing near to this presence of God may be a little painful in the beginning, but it produces marvelous effects in the soul when it is faithfully practiced. It draws down in abundance the graces of the Lord and carries the soul without effort to that pure gazing, that loving sight of God present everywhere, which is the holiest, the firmest, the easiest, and the most powerful manner of prayer.

Notice, please, that to arrive at this state, we take for granted the putting to death of the senses. A soul that still takes some pleasure in worldly things cannot wholly enjoy this divine presence; for to be with God, one must absolutely turn away from the satisfaction of worldly pleasures.

Spiritual Maxims

Practicing the presence of God strengthens us in hope. Our hope increases in proportion to our knowledge—to the extent that our faith penetrates by remaining close to Jesus into the revelations of the Trinity, and to the extent that it discovers in God a beauty infinitely surpassing not only that of the earth, but even that of the saints in heaven and the angels. Our hope increases and grows stronger, and is reassured and sustained by an intimacy with God that the soul expects to enjoy and that in some degree it tastes.

Spiritual Maxims

By this interior gaze, the soul comes to know God so completely that it passes almost its whole life in continual acts of love, adoration, contrition, confidence, thanksgiving, offering, petition, and all the most excellent virtues. Sometimes our life even becomes one single act that does not end, because the soul is always engaged in the act of remaining in this divine presence.

Spiritual Maxims

In order to be with God throughout the day, it is not necessary to stay in church all the time. We can make our heart like a little chapel into which we retire from time to time to converse with him gently, humbly, and lovingly. Everyone is capable of these familiar conversations with God—some more, others less. Our Father knows what we can do. Let us begin. Perhaps he is only waiting for a generous resolution on our part. Courage, for no matter how old we are, we only have but a short time to live! I am nearly eighty years old. Let us live and die in God's presence. Suffering will always be sweet to us when we are with him. But without him, the greatest pleasures will be a cruel torment to us. May Jesus be blessed in everything! Amen.

Fourth Letter

The most holy and important practice in the spiritual life is the presence of God—that is, every moment to take great pleasure that God is with you. In doing so, we speak humbly and converse with him lovingly during all seasons, in every minute, without rule or measure. Above all, we are with him in times of temptations, sorrows, dryness, even of infidelities and sin.

Spiritual Maxims

It is critical that we place all of our confidence in God and rid ourselves of all other cares—even of many special devotions which, although they may be good, have been undertaken rashly. After all, these devotions are only a means to an end. Since by this practice of the presence of God, we are with him who is our end, it is useless for us to return to the means. We must continue our communion of love with him, remaining in his holy presence: sometimes by an act of adoration, of praise, of desire; sometimes by an act of offering, of thanksgiving; and in all the ways that our spirit can invent.

Third Letter

I cannot understand how Christians can be content without practicing the presence of God. As for me, I draw close to him in the depth and center of my soul as much as I can, and when I am with him like that, I am afraid of nothing.

Third Letter

This is my typical practice since I have been a monk. Even though I have practiced staying in God's presence only with cowardice and many failures, still I have received enormous advantages from it. I am sure that this can only be attributed to God's mercy and goodness, since we can do nothing without him, and I even less than most people. When we are faithful to holding ourselves in his holy presence and to considering him as always before us, this prevents us from offending him and from doing anything that might displease him—at least voluntarily. It is because we know that he is with us that we take a holy freedom to ask him for the graces we need. Finally, because we repeat these acts of turning to Jesus hour by hour or minute by minute, we make them more familiar to ourselves and the presence of God becomes a natural thing.

Twelfth Letter

Fixing our thoughts on God throughout the day does not harm the body. Still, it is proper to deprive the body from time to time, and even often, of many little pleasures, even though they may be permissible. For God does not allow a person who wishes to belong entirely to him to take pleasure in anything other than him. That makes complete sense.

I do not say that for this reason a person must torment himself. No, God must be served with holy freedom. We should labor faithfully, without distress or anxiety, gently and calmly recalling our spirit to God as many times as we find it distracted from him.

Third Letter

I have given up all my private devotions and prayers that are not required, and spend my time only with holding myself ever in his holy presence. This I do by a simple attention and a general, loving gaze upon God, which I call "the actual presence of God" or, better yet, "a silent and secret conversation of the soul with God." This closeness rarely ceases. I experience such contentment and joy, interiorly and even exteriorly, that in order to stop it and prevent it from becoming apparent to those around me, I am forced to act like a child, and I seem more like a fool than a devoted lover of God.

Fifth Letter

The typical state I find myself in is this simple attention, this loving gaze upon God, in which I feel greater joy and peace than a baby feels at the breast of his mother. If I dared to use the expression, I would willingly call this state "the breast of God," because of the inexpressible sweetness that I taste and experience in it.

If sometimes—because of preoccupation or weakness—I turn away, I am immediately recalled by interior emotions of the heart, which are so delightful that I am embarrassed to mention them.

Fifth Letter

I know that some Christians consider this state as laziness, deception, and self-love. I reply that it is a holy laziness and a blessed self-love, if the soul were capable of them. However, when it is in this state of rest, the soul cannot be disturbed by the devotions it used to make, which were then its support but now would only harm rather than help it.

I cannot permit anyone to call this state a deception, since the soul is enjoying God and does not desire anything but him. If this is deception in me, then God himself must remedy it. Let the Lord do with me what he pleases, for I want nothing but Jesus and to be all his.

Fifth Letter

If sometimes we are a little distant from the Lord's presence, God immediately makes himself felt within our hearts to recall us back to him. This happens most frequently when we are most occupied in outside duties. We can respond with faithfulness to the interior drawing of the Holy Spirit, either by raising our hearts to God, or by a gentle and loving look, or by some words that love prompts at these meetings. For example, you might say, "My God, I am all yours. Do with me as you will." Then it seems as if the Spirit of love, contenting himself with this little prayer, goes to sleep again and rests in the depth and center of our souls. Experiencing God's presence makes us so certain that God is always in the depth of our hearts that we cannot even doubt it, no matter what troubles come.

First Letter

Continual conversation with God is sweeter and more delightful than any other way of living in this world. Only those who practice and taste God's presence can understand this joy. However, I do not advise you to practice it for this motive. We do not seek consolations in this exercise, but we do it out of love for the Lord, and simply because he wills it.

If I were a preacher, I would preach nothing else than the practice of the presence of God; and if I were a director of souls, I would recommend to everyone that they continually converse with God, because I believe it is so vital and even easy to practice.

Second Letter

What can be more pleasing to God than to stop whatever we are doing a thousand times a day to worship him in our hearts? It would only be more pleasing to him if we could destroy the self-centered love that exists among us, and by which we are gradually freed through these interior visits to God. In short, we cannot give God greater pledges of our loyalty than by renouncing and despising the flesh, the world, and the devil a thousand times, so that we can enjoy one single moment with the Creator.

Spiritual Maxims

How happy we would be, if we could find the treasure of which the gospel speaks! Everything else would seem to us as nothing. As the gospel is infinite, the more one explores it, the more riches does he find. Let us constantly look for the treasures hidden in the gospel and not grow weary until we have found them.

Sixth Letter

People would be surprised if they knew what one's soul says to God sometimes. He seems to be so well pleased with these conversations that he permits everything to the soul, provided that it always wills to dwell with him in its depths. As if the Lord feared that the soul might love human affairs more than himself, he takes care to give it all that it could desire, so that it often finds within itself a very savory and delicious refreshment. This occurs even though a person may never have desired or sought such a grace in any way, and may not have contributed anything to it except for having received it freely.

Spiritual Maxims

I know that there are not many people who attain such constant union with God the Father; it is a grace given by God since this simple gaze is a gift of his generous hand. But I will say, for the consolation of those who wish to embrace this holy practice, that he usually gives it to those who open themselves to it; and if God does not, one can at least, with the help of his manifold graces, acquire by the practice of the presence of God a method and state of prayer that very closely approach this simple gazing upon him.

Spiritual Maxims

Once again, let us enter the interior place of our hearts. Time presses on, and there is no way to make up for lost opportunities. Each of us must persevere and draw near to God. I am sure you have taken such wise measures that you will never be surprised. I praise your efforts—for that is our purpose in life. However, we must always labor to stay close to Jesus, because when we do not advance, we retreat. Yet, those who have the wind of the Holy Spirit sail even while they are asleep. When we find the vessels of our souls tossed by the winds or storms of life, let us awaken the Lord who is sleeping in the boat, and he will swiftly calm the sea.

First Letter

2

A Lively Faith

The first fruit that a person receives from the practice of the presence of God is that their faith is livelier and more active in all the circumstances of life. This is particularly true in times of need, since this practice easily obtains for us grace in our temptations and in the inevitable dealings that we must have with other people. The soul, accustomed to the practice of faith, by a simple act of memory, sees and feels God present; it recalls him easily and effectively, and obtains what it needs. One might say that the soul possesses something approaching the state of the Blessed: The more it advances, the more lively its faith becomes, and finally it grows so penetrating that it might almost say, "I no longer know by faith, but I see and experience God's very presence and love."

Spiritual Maxims

I know that the beginning of practicing God's presence is very difficult and that we must act purely in faith. We know also that we can accomplish all things with the grace of the Lord. God does not refuse his anointings to those who ask persistently. Knock at the door of God's heart. Persevere in knocking. I promise you that he will open it in time, if you do not stop trying, and he will suddenly give you all that he has delayed for many years. Pray to him for me as I do for you, for I hope to see him very soon. I am wholly yours in Our Lord.

Fifteenth Letter

During my first years as a monk, in my daily prayers, I used to focus my thoughts on death, judgment, hell, heaven, and my sins. I continued this way for several years. I sought to stay focused the rest of the day and even during my work with God's presence. I always believed that the Lord remained near me in the depth of my heart. This heightened my experience of the Lord so much that faith alone was able to satisfy me in coming to know him even more.

Fifth Letter

Gradually, I did the same thing during my prayer time, which gave me great sweetness and joy. I will tell you, however, that during the first ten years I suffered very much. I feared that I did not belong to God as much as I desired. My past sins always seemed present before my eyes. Even the great graces that God gave me were a source of my trials. During this whole time, I used to fall to temptation often. It seemed to me that my friends, my thoughts, and even God were against me. Faith alone was on my side. I was sometimes troubled with the thought that I presumed that I could aspire to be suddenly at a point of holiness that others reach only with difficulty. At other times, I thought that I was willfully destroying myself, that there was no salvation for me.

Fifth Letter

did not expect anything more than to end my days in this distress and anxiety, (which did not at all decrease my confidence in God and served only to increase my faith), when suddenly I found myself wholly changed. My soul, which until then was always troubled, felt a profound interior peace, as if it had found its center and place of rest.

Since that time, I have been working before God simply, in faith, with humility and love—and I try carefully to do nothing that could displease him. I hope that, when I have done what I can, he will do with me as he pleases.

Fifth Letter

Let us go beyond seeking or loving God for the sake of the graces that he has given us, however wonderful they may be, or for those that he may give us in the future. These blessings will never carry us so near to him as faith does with a simple gaze. Let us seek him often through this virtue. He is within us—let us not seek him elsewhere. Aren't we rude, and even guilty, of leaving him alone, absorbed in a thousand trifles that displease and maybe offend him? He endures them, but we should be afraid that someday they may cost us a great deal.

Sixteenth Letter

I am very close to the day when I will see God, when I will render an account to him. If I see God for just one minute, the sufferings of purgatory would be sweet to me, even if they last until the end of the world. What comforts me now is that I see God by faith; and I see him in a way that might sometimes make me say: "I no longer believe, but I see, I experience what faith teaches us." With this assurance and this practice of faith, I will live and die with the Lord.

Eleventh Letter

God has infinite treasures to give us, and yet a small sense of his presence that lasts only a minute seems to satisfy us. Through our blindness, we tie God's hands and dam up the river of his grace. Yet when he finds our soul penetrated with a lively faith, he pours on us graces in abundance. God's grace is like a torrent, held back forcibly from its normal course, but when it finds an open heart, gushes out exuberantly.

Yes, often we stop this torrent because we place so little value on it. Let us not stop the Lord's grace any longer. Let us enter into our hearts, break this dam, give light to grace, and make up for lost time. Perhaps we do not have long to live and death is on our heels.

First Letter

In order to become entirely united to the will of God, we only have to grow in faith, hope, and charity. Everything else is unimportant. We should not dwell on other spiritual things but view them as a bridge we must cross very quickly in order to lose ourselves in confidence and love for Jesus, our final destination.

Fourth Conversation

All things are possible for those who believe. Even more is possible for those who hope, still more to those who love and, most of all, to those who practice and persevere in all of these virtues.

Fourth Conversation

Brother Lawrence urged us to enliven our faith. What a pitiful thing that we should have so little faith! Instead of taking our relationship with God as a foundation and guide, we amuse ourselves with petty devotions that change every day. This road of faith is the spirit of the church, and it can lead us to perfection.

First Conversation

He said we would need to be filled with faith in order to endure the dry times through which our Father tests our love for him. When we are full of faith and trust, we can resign and abandon ourselves to the Lord. This is a great help for our journey.

First Conversation

3

Consider Who We Are

When we begin the spiritual life, we should fundamentally consider who we are. If we do, we will find ourselves deserving of all contempt, unworthy of the name of Christian, rightfully subject to all sorts of miseries, and to the many accidents that easily upset us. So many things make us unstable in our health, in our moods, in our interior and exterior dispositions. In short, God wills to humble us through many sufferings and situations, both those within our minds as well as those outside our control. After that, should we be surprised when we encounter pains, temptations, opposition, and contradiction from our neighbor? Shouldn't we, rather, submit to these situations and bear them as long as God wills, since they help us draw close to God?

Fourth Conversation

All worship and adoration should be made by faith, believing that God really is in our hearts. We need to adore Jesus, love him, and serve him in spirit and in truth. Know that he sees all that passes and will pass within us and in every person. Understand that while he needs nothing, we depend on him for everything. God is infinite in his perfection and worthy by his sovereign rule. All that we are and all that exists in heaven and on earth, God can dispose of at his good pleasure during time and eternity. In justice, we owe him all our thoughts, all our words, and all our actions. Examine whether we pay this debt to him.

Spiritual Maxims

Unquestionably we must believe that it is good for us and agreeable to God to sacrifice ourselves for him. We must believe that it is normal for his Divine Providence to abandon us to all sorts of states, to suffer all kinds of pains, miseries, and temptations for the love of God and as long as he pleases. Why? Because without this submission of heart and mind to the will of God, devoted obedience and spiritual maturity cannot be attained.

Spiritual Maxims

Brother rarely had a problem with being over-scrupulous with sin. "When I realize that I have sinned," he told me, "I agree and realize, 'That is my nature. The only thing I know how to do is sin.' When I don't sin, I thank my heavenly Father for his grace and acknowledge that this grace comes from him alone."

Second Conversation

Whenever he sinned, he did nothing else but admit his fault, saying to God: "I cannot do anything other than fall, if I am apart from you. You must stop me from falling and correct whatever is not right." After admitting his sin, he did not worry about it anymore.

Second Conversation

Knowing that God should be loved in everything and working to fulfill this duty, Brother Lawrence said he did not need a spiritual director but only a confessor so that he might receive absolution for his faults. He declared that he did indeed perceive his faults and was never surprised at them, but that he confessed them to Jesus and did not make excuses for his failings. Afterwards, he re-entered peacefully into his usual efforts of love and adoration.

Second Conversation

Instead of being astonished at the misery and sins that he heard mentioned everyday, Brother Lawrence was actually surprised that they were not more common, considering the evil every sinner is capable of. He prayed for sinners, but since he knew that the Lord could remedy the problem of evil whenever he chose, Brother did not worry any more about it.

First Conversation

4

The Sweetness of Suffering

God knows perfectly well what we need, and everything he does is for our good. If we knew how much he loves us, we would always be ready to receive both sweet blessings or bitter circumstances. Even the most painful and hardest things would be sweet and agreeable to us. The harshest trials generally are not unbearable. But the view we take of them makes them seem unbearable. When we are convinced that the hand of God is upon us, that it is a Father full of love who places us in states of humiliation, sorrow and suffering, all the bitterness is taken away from them, and our pain seems sweet.

Sixteenth Letter

How sweet it can be to suffer with God! However great our sufferings may be, accept them with love. It is a paradise to suffer and to be with Jesus. Besides, if we wish to enjoy even in this life the peace of God, we must get into the habit of a familiar, humble, and loving conversation with him. We must prevent our minds from wandering, no matter what we are doing, for we must make our hearts a spiritual temple for him, in which we adore him without end. We must watch over ourselves constantly, so as not to do or say or think anything that can displease him. When we are thus engaged with God, sufferings will be nothing more than sweetness, balm, and consolation.

Fifteenth Letter

Don't beg God to be delivered from your physical pain. Ask him for the strength to suffer courageously for his love for as long as he pleases. I know that these prayers don't come naturally to us, but they are very pleasing to God and sweet to those who love him. Love sweetens pain, and when one loves God, one suffers for him with joy and courage. Pray like this, I urge you. Console yourself with God who is the sole remedy for all our ills. He is the Father of the afflicted, always ready to aid us. He loves us infinitely more than we think. Love him in return. Do not search any longer for any other comfort than God himself, and I hope that you will receive his consolation very soon.

Fourteenth Letter

I am so sorry to see you suffering for so long. What sweetens my compassion for you is that I believe that suffering is proof of God's love for you. Consider struggles in this way and they will be easy for you to bear. My thought is that you should leave all human remedies and abandon yourself entirely to Divine Providence. Perhaps God is only waiting for this abandonment and a perfect confidence in him to heal you. In spite of all your care, the remedies do not have the effect they should. On the contrary, the illness grows worse. It would be no longer tempting God to abandon yourself into his hands and expect everything from him.

Fourteenth Letter

Take courage, my friend. Continually offer the Lord your pain. Ask him for the strength to endure. More than anything, get used to conversing often with him, and remember him as often as you can. Adore him when you are ill. Offer any suffering you have to him from time to time. And when your pain is at its worst, beg him humbly and lovingly, as a child does of his good father. This will help you conform to his holy will with the help of his grace. I will help you by my poor, weak prayers.

God has many means of drawing us to him. He hides himself from us sometimes, but faith alone, which will not fail us, must be our support and the foundation of our confidence, which should be wholly in God.

Thirteenth Letter

If we were really in the habit of practicing the presence of God, all sicknesses of the body would seem small to us. Often God permits that we suffer a little to purify our souls and urges us to dwell with him alone. I cannot understand how a person who walks with God and wants only him can be capable of pain. I have even enough experience myself to be sure of this.

Thirteenth Letter

Be content with the place and condition in which God has placed you. However happy you think I am, I envy you. Sorrows and suffering can be a paradise if I suffer with God. On the other hand, the greatest pleasure in the world would be like hell to me, if I tasted them apart from Jesus. My whole consolation would be to suffer with him.

Eleventh Letter

I would like you to consider that God is often nearer to us in seasons of illness and infirmity than when we enjoy perfect health. Seek healing from the divine Physician. As far as I can understand the matter, he wishes to heal you himself. Place all your confidence in him; you will soon see the results.

Whatever medicines you use, they will be effective only insofar as the Lord blesses them. When the sufferings come from God, he alone can heal them. He sometimes gives us disorders of the body in order to heal those of the soul. Console yourself with the sovereign Physician of souls and bodies.

Eleventh Letter

Blessed are they who suffer with him. Get used to suffering with Christ. Ask God for the strength to suffer whatever he wishes and for as long as he judges it necessary. The world does not understand suffering with Jesus, and I am not surprised by it, for they suffer like people of the world and not like Christians. They look upon sickness as afflictions of nature and not as graces of God. Therefore, they find in sickness only the severity and harshness of nature. But God's children who consider all pain and suffering as coming from the hand of God, as a means for his mercy and salvation, can find in them much sweetness and consolation.

Eleventh Letter

I do not ask God to deliver you from the suffering and pain of life, but I do beg him urgently that he may give you the strength and patience to suffer as long as he desires. Console yourself with Jesus who keeps you crucified with him. He will set you free when he thinks it is the right time.

Eleventh Letter

We have a Father infinitely good, who knows what he is doing. I have always thought that he would want me to suffer great afflictions. He comes in his good time, and when I least expect it. Hope in him today more than ever. Thank him for the graces he is giving you, particularly for the strength and patience he gives you in your trials, for it is proof of his care. Console yourself with him and thank him for everything.

Seventh Letter

I don't know what God wants to do with me, for I am more peaceful each day. Everybody suffers and I, who should be doing rigorous penances, feel so much joy so continually that I have trouble containing my happiness.

I would willingly ask God for a share in your sufferings, if I did not know my weakness. My weakness is so great that, if the Lord left me alone for one moment, I would be the most miserable of all creatures. However, I do not know how he could leave me alone, since faith draws me to his presence so easily. The Lord never departs from us unless we go away first. Let us be afraid to leave him, let us be always with him, let us live and die with him. Pray to him for me, and I will for you.

Thirteenth Letter

5

Crying Out to God for Help

We must carefully examine the virtues that are the most important for us to have, those most difficult for us to acquire, the sins into which we most frequently fall, and the most usual and unavoidable occasions of our falls. During times of struggle, we should cry out to God for help, entirely confident, and remain steadfast in his glorious presence. We should adore him humbly, declare to him our misery and weakness, and lovingly beg for his grace. As we do this, we will find in him all virtues, even though we possess none of them on our own merit.

Spiritual Maxims

It's impossible to avoid the dangers and pitfalls that are so common in life without the Lord's continual help. So let us ask him for it ceaselessly. How can we ask for it without being in his presence? How can we think of him often, if we are not in the holy habit of doing so, which requires practice? You might say that I am always telling you the same thing. It is true, for I do not know any way more appropriate or easy than this. And as I do not practice any other way of prayer, I recommend this to everybody. We have to know a person before we can love him, and in order to know the Lord we must think of him often. Even when we do love him, we will also think of him very often, for our heart is where our treasure is!

Ninth Letter

Ah, if we only knew our desperate need for God's grace and help, we would never lose him from our sight for a moment. Trust me. Right now, make a holy and firm decision never to flee from him on purpose, and to live the rest of your days in his holy presence, longing for his love and deprived, if it is God's will, of everything else in heaven and earth. Set your hand to the task. If you fix your eyes on God as you should, be assured that you will soon see God's grace changing your life. I will help you with my prayers, poor though they may be.

Second Letter

Brother Lawrence told me that he now could have no thoughts or desires except of God. Whenever he faced some other thought or a temptation coming on, he experienced the Holy Spirit's prompt assistance. To grow in receiving the Lord's help, he sometimes even allowed the thoughts to continue and when it was time, he appealed to God and found that the temptation vanished right away.

In the same way, when he had business to accomplish, he did not prepare in advance. When the time came to take action, he looked at God, as in a clear mirror. There he found what he needed to do at that present moment. Before this experience of the swift help of God in his affairs, he did worry about such matters in advance. But later, whenever he had business to do, he did so without any concern, fear, or worry.

Third Conversation

Brother Lawrence pointed out that we must act very simply with God and speak to him frankly, asking his help with problems and concerns as they came up. He said God never failed to pour out grace, as he had often experienced. He had been told, a few days before, to go into Burgundy in order to get supplies of wine. This was very difficult for him because, besides the fact that he had little business sense, he was lame in one leg. He couldn't even walk on the boat without hitting up against the barrels. However, he was not worried about his awkwardness, any more than about his whole purchase of wine. He simply knew that it was the Lord's affair, after which he found that everything turned out fine.

Second Conversation

In the beginning of the spiritual life, we must be faithful, he said, both in our actions and in renouncing our will. After that, there are only indescribable delights. In difficulties, we simply need to turn to Jesus Christ and pray for his grace, which makes everything easy.

Third Conversation

Brother had expected that after the Lord had blessed him with consolation and comfort, he would then have his share of pain and suffering. However, he never worried about this, knowing well that since he could do nothing by his own human strength, God would not fail to anoint him with the strength to bear any struggle. He had always turned to God when he was trying to practice some virtue, saying to the Lord, "My God, I am not able to stay faithful, if you do not help me." Immediately, he was given enough strength, and even more.

Second Conversation

We should ask for God's grace with great confidence. We ought not to pay attention to our racing thoughts, but trust in the infinite goodness of our Lord. Brother Lawrence said that God would never fail to give us his grace every time we cried out. He himself was acutely aware of this. He only sinned at those times when he became distracted from God's company or when he had forgotten to ask for the Lord's help.

Fourth Conversation

The more a person aspires to high perfection, the more dependent he is upon the grace of God. God's help is so much more needed at each moment, because without it the soul can do nothing. Our enemies—the world, the flesh, and the devil—together wage such fierce and continual war upon the soul that without actual help and humble, necessary dependence, these adversaries would drag the soul down in spite of our efforts to stand firm. This dependence seems hard to nature, but God's grace within us is pleased with our weak condition and takes refuge as we are weak and needy before the Lord.

Spiritual Maxims

6

The Fire of Holy Love

Maintaining intimacy with Jesus inspires in our wills a contempt for created things and sets this will aglow with the fire of holy love because the soul is always with God, who is a consuming fire and reduces into ashes whatever can be opposed to him. The soul, on fire with the Spirit, can no longer live except in the presence of God, a presence that produces in the heart a holy zeal, an urgency about spiritual things, and a violent desire to experience God, who is loved, known, served, and adored by all creatures.

Spiritual Maxims

When I saw Brother Lawrence for the first time, he told me that the Lord had given him an extraordinary grace in his conversion, before he had entered the monastery when he was 18 years old. One winter day, he was gazing at a tree stripped of its leaves. He realized that some time later these leaves would appear again, along with flowers and then fruits. At that instant, he was so profoundly impressed with the Father's power and providence that this image was burned into his soul and detached him entirely from the world. It gave him such a love of God that Brother Lawrence could not say whether it had ever grown greater in the more than 40 years since then.

First Conversation

We should realize that this conversation with God occurs in the depth and center of a person. It is there that the soul speaks to God, heart to heart, and always in a great and profound peace that the soul enjoys in God. Everything that happens outside is to the soul only a blaze of straw that goes out while it is catching fire, and scarcely ever disturbs its interior peace.

To return to our presence of God, I say that this gentle and loving gazing at God without notice generates in the soul a divine fire that so enflames a person with the love of God that he is obliged to do many external things to temper it.

Spiritual Maxims

Is it not proper that the heart, which brings life to all the other parts of the body, should be the first and the last to love God, whether upon beginning or ending all our spiritual or bodily actions, and generally in all the deeds of our lives? It is in the heart that we must carefully produce this little interior glance, which must be done as I have already said, without trouble and without contriving to make it easier.

Spiritual Maxims

Three kinds of unions exist: the first habitual, the second virtual, and the third actual. Habitual union occurs when one is united to God only by grace. Virtual union exists when, beginning an action by which one unites oneself to God, a person remains united to him by virtue of this action, as long as it lasts. Actual union is the most perfect kind. Wholly spiritual as it is, it makes its movement felt, because the soul is not asleep as in the other unions, but powerfully excited.

Its operation is livelier than that of fire and shines more brightly than the sun on a clear day. However, one can be mistaken in this sentiment. Actual union is not a simple expression of the heart. It is an ineffable state of the soul—gentle, peaceful, devout, respectful, humble, loving, and very simple—that urges and presses it to love God, to adore him, even to embrace him with inexpressible tenderness such as only experience can make us imagine.

Spiritual Maxims

Everyone must admit that God is far beyond our comprehension and that to unite oneself to him intimately, we must put to death in our wills all sorts of tastes and pleasures of mind and body, so that being thus set free, our wills can love God in everything. For if the will can in some way comprehend God, it can be only by love. There is a great difference between the preferences and feelings of the will and the acts of the same will, since the preferences and feelings of the will are limited in the soul, while an act of the will, which is properly love, finds God as its purpose and goal.

Spiritual Maxims

He remarked that people performed penances and other devotions, but they neglected love, which is the purpose of such exercises. This was easy to see in their actions and it was the reason that they possessed so little solid virtue.

Neither talent or education were needed, he declared, to go to God—only a heart resolved to think solely about the Lord, and to love no one but him.

Third Conversation

Let us spend all of our time experiencing God. The more one knows him, the more one desires to know him. As love is usually measured by knowledge, the greater the width and depth of the knowledge, the greater will be the love. If love is great, we will love equally during times of sorrow and of joy.

Sixteenth Letter

He remarked that he was not bold enough to ask God for penances and that he did not even want to do any, although he knew he deserved many. When God sent him something to endure, he would also give grace. All penances and other exercises, he thought, only served to lead us to union with God through love. After considering the matter thoroughly, he found it much shorter to go straight to the Lord by a continual practice of love, in doing everything for the love of God.

Second Conversation

Brother Lawrence said that for years, he had suffered greatly in spirit, believing that he would not be saved. No one in the world could have changed this opinion. However, he thought about it in this way: "I became a monk only for the love of God. I have tried to act only for him. Whether or not I will be saved, I want to continue to act purely for the love of God. I will have at least this much good—that until I die, I will do what I can to love him."

This distress had lasted four years, during which time he had suffered intensely! After that, he thought neither of heaven or of hell. His whole life was simply freedom of the spirit and continual rejoicing in the Lord Jesus. He placed his sins between God and himself, as if to tell the Father that he did not deserve any grace. But this did not hinder the Lord from overwhelming Brother with his grace and love.

Second Conversation

Brother Lawrence said he had always guided himself by love. He had no other interest and he didn't worry whether or not he would be saved. However, after determining that he would do everything out of love for God, he found himself quite peaceful. He was even content when he could pick up a blade of grass from the ground out of love for Jesus, since he sought his face alone and not his gifts.

Second Conversation

7

Before God in Prayer

I do not advise you to say many words in prayer, since long discourse is often an occasion for the mind to wander. In prayer, hold yourself before God like a poor mute man and a paralytic at the door of a rich man, and spend your time keeping your soul in the presence of the Lord. If it wanders and withdraws from him at times, do not be upset. These things may distract the soul, but the will must bring it back gently. If you persevere in this way, God will have mercy on you.

Eighth Letter

One way of recalling the mind easily during prayer and of keeping it more tranquil is not to let your mind race during the day, but to hold it close to the presence of God. Being in the habit of coming back to him from time to time, you will find it easy to remain peaceful during your prayer time, or at least to bring your mind back from distractions.

Eighth Letter

You have told me nothing new, for you are not the only one affected by distractions. Our minds are extremely flighty. However, our wills are in charge of all our thoughts and desires and so must recall the mind and carry it to God, its true goal.

When the mind, which has not been subdued early on, has fallen into some bad habits of wandering and wasting time, these habits are difficult to conquer and ordinarily drag us down to the things of earth. I think that a remedy for that is to confess our faults and to humble ourselves before God.

Eighth Letter

It was a great mistake, Brother Lawrence said, to believe that the time for prayer should be different from any other time. We are obligated to be united to God by work, during working hours, as by prayer at the time we set aside for prayer.

Fourth Conversation

Prayer to him was simply experiencing the presence of God. His soul ignored everything else but love, all other thoughts as if asleep. Outside of this time, he found scarcely any difference, keeping himself always near to God to praise him and bless him with all of his power. He thus spent his life in continual joy, although he hoped that God would give him something to suffer when he was strong enough to endure it.

Fourth Conversation

At the beginning of his conversion, he had often spent the whole time of prayer in rejecting distractions and falling into them again. Brother said that he had never been able to meditate according to a method, as others did. In the beginning, he had prayed aloud for some time, but afterwards he could not recall what had happened.

Second Conversation

Brother Lawrence said his time of prayer was no different from any other time. He made his retreats when it was time, but he did not desire them or ask for them, since his greatest work did not distract him from the Lord.

Second Conversation

8

Absolute Abandonment

Brother Lawrence remarked that we must give ourselves entirely to God in absolute abandonment, in both everyday and spiritual affairs. We are to seek happiness in doing the Father's will, whether the Lord leads us through times of suffering or through times of comfort and consolation. It should be all the same to those who have truly abandoned themselves to God.

First Conversation

In order to abandon ourselves as much as Jesus desires, we must watch carefully our impulses, which affect every area of our lives—spiritual matters as well as the most common things. God shines his light on these impulses for those who genuinely desire to belong to him.

First Conversation

Brother knew that the trust we place in God the Father gives great honor to him and brings us abundant graces. It was impossible, Brother Lawrence said, for God to deceive us or to permit us to suffer for very long when our hearts and minds are totally abandoned to him and resolved to endure every situation for him.

Third Conversation

Even though he expected that the future would bring some great suffering of body or soul, Brother Lawrence said his worst trial would be to lose the Father's presence, which he had felt for such a long time. However, the goodness of God made him absolutely certain that the Lord would never leave him entirely. He knew that God would give him the strength to endure whatever evil might come to him. With this assurance, he was not afraid of anything.

In desiring to die and to lose himself for the love of God, he had no apprehension or fear. Entire abandonment to God was the sure road on which we would always have enough light to guide us.

Third Conversation

Brother Lawrence said he was not worried about death, or about his sins, or of heaven, or even of hell. He thought only of doing little things out of love for God, since he couldn't do great things. After having walked in God's will, anything that happened to him during the day would not bother him. It was simply God's will. Nothing in the world, not even being skinned alive, could compare to the interior suffering and joys he experienced as he grew in the spiritual life. Therefore, he didn't worry about anything. He didn't fear anything. And he asked God for nothing except that he would not disobey him.

Second Conversation

I do not know what will become of me. It seems that peace of soul and a restful spirit come to me while I am asleep. If I were capable of suffering, there would be none for me to have. If I were allowed, I would willingly console myself with the thought that there is a purgatory, in which I hope to suffer for the reparation of my sins. I do not know what God has in store for me; I am in such great tranquillity that I fear nothing. What could I fear, when I am with my God? I stay there as much as I can. May he be blessed for everything! Amen.

Sixth Letter

Sometimes, during my hours of prayer, I picture myself as a piece of stone before a sculptor who intends to make a statue out of it. Presenting myself like this before the Lord, I beg him to form in my soul his perfect image and make me wholly like Christ. At other times, as soon as possible, I feel my whole mind and heart rise without care or effort and remain suspended, fixed in God at its center and place of rest.

Fifth Letter

Once and for all, let us begin to be his entirely. Let us banish from our hearts and our souls all that is not Jesus. He wishes to rule our hearts and minds alone; let us ask him for this grace. If we do what we can on our part, we will soon see within us the change that we are hoping for. I hope from his mercy the grace to see him in a few days. Let us pray to him for each other.

Sixteenth Letter

I feel no anxiety or doubt about my condition, because I have no other wish than to do what God wants. I try in all things to do his will, and I would not wish to lift a straw from the ground against his order, nor for any other motive than the pure love of him.

Fifth Letter

9

Finding God in Our Work

He said our holiness depends not on changing jobs, but on doing for God what we usually do for ourselves. It was a pity, he thought, to see how many people mistake the means (our work) for the end (our walk in faith) by becoming too engrossed in our daily responsibilities, which we often perform imperfectly and primarily for human respect.

He found no better way to approach God than through the ordinary tasks assigned to him. When Brother did his duties, he avoided as much as possible all human respect and did them solely out of love for God.

Fourth Conversation

We should never, Brother Lawrence remarked, grow weary of doing the smallest things out of love of God. The Father does not regard the greatness of the work, but its love. We must not be surprised at failing often in the beginning. In the end, resting in the Lord's love would become a habit that would allow us to perform our actions effortlessly and with great pleasure.

Fourth Conversation

Brother Lawrence hated working in the kitchen, but had gotten used to doing everything for the love of God. He asked for the Spirit's help on every occasion while he worked, and had developed a great proficiency during the fifteen years he spent in the kitchen. Later, he worked in the shoe repair shop, which he liked very much, but he said he was ready to leave this job if God desired. He merely rejoiced in being able to do little things for the love of God.

Second Conversation

When outside business diverted his attention a little from pondering the Lord, Jesus sent him some revelation that took possession of his soul. This gave him so strong a sense of God that it set him on fire and he cried out. He even felt overwhelming impulses to sing and leap about like a crazy man.

Brother Lawrence said he was much more united to God during his ordinary activities than when he left them to make his spiritual exercises and retreats. These retreats usually left him with a great spiritual dryness.

Third Conversation

He said he couldn't recall most of the things he did during the day. He paid almost no attention even while he did them, and even after leaving the dinner table, he did not know what he had eaten. Abiding in simplicity before God, he performed his responsibilities out of love for the Father. He thanked the Lord for directing his actions, and made many other offerings of love to God. All this was done very calmly, in a way that kept him in the loving presence of the Father.

Third Conversation

All our actions should be undertaken with deliberation and care, without being impulsive or hasty, for these show a disordered spirit. We must work gently, calmly, and lovingly with God, and beg him to accept our work. By constantly staying close to God, we will crush the devil's head and make his weapons fall from his hands.

Spiritual Maxims

You must try continually to make all of your actions, without distinction, a sort of little conversation with God—not in a rehearsed way but just as they happen, with purity and simplicity of heart.

Spiritual Maxims

Remember my advice to you to think of the Lord, day and night, in all your duties and routines, even during your recreation. Your heavenly Father is always near you and with you. Do not leave him alone. You would never be so rude as to leave a friend who was visiting you. Why abandon God and leave him alone? Do not forget him! Think of him often, adore him continually, live and die with him. That is the real business of a Christian; in a word, it is our profession. If we do not know it, we must learn. I will help you with my prayers.

Tenth Letter

10

The Merciful King

I believe I should tell you how I view myself before God, whom I envision as my king. I consider myself to be the most miserable of men, wounded and stinking, who has committed all sorts of crimes against his king. I am overwhelmed by remorse. I confess to him all my evil deeds. I beg his pardon for my sins, and I abandon myself into his hands, to do with me whatever he pleases.

This King, full of goodness and mercy, far from chastising me, embraces me lovingly, invites me to eat at his table, serves me with his own hands, gives me the keys of his treasury, and treats me in every way as his favorite child. He speaks with me and enjoys my company endlessly in a thousand ways, without speaking of pardoning me, nor criticizing old habits. Although I urge him to do with me as he wills, I find myself weak and miserable, yet caressed by God. That is how I look upon myself from time to time in his holy presence.

Fifth Letter

I know that you will tell me that I am having an easy time in life because I eat and drink at the table of the Lord. You are right. But don't you think it would be a great embarrassment to the greatest criminal in the world to eat at the table of the King, to be served by his hands, without being assured of his pardon? I think such a sinner would feel mortified, which only hope in the mercy of his King could alleviate! So I can assure you that, whatever solace I feel in drinking and eating at the table of my King, my sins, which are constantly before my eyes, as well as the uncertainty of my forgiveness, torment me. But even this suffering draws me closer to God

Eleventh Letter

Our only purpose in this life is to please God. What can all the rest be, except foolishness and vanity? You and I have spent more than forty years following the Lord. Have we used these years to love and serve our Father? I am filled with shame and embarrassment when I reflect, on the one hand, on the many graces that the Lord has given me and constantly continues to give me, and on the other, on the poor use that I have made of them and my small progress in growing in holiness.

Ninth Letter

Because the Lord is so merciful, he has given us a little more time. Therefore, let us begin all over again and make up for any lost opportunities. Let us return with absolute confidence to this kind Father, who is always ready to receive us lovingly into his arms. Because we love him generously, let us renounce everything that is not of him, since he deserves much more than that. Let's think of him continually and place all our confidence in him. I have no doubt that we will quickly experience the effects of being in his presence and feel the abundance of his graces, with which we can do everything—and without which we can commit only sin.

Ninth Letter

Brother felt that even if we should do all possible penances, if they were devoid of love, they would not serve to lessen a single sin. Without worrying, we should wait peacefully as the blood of Jesus Christ deals with our sins. We ought only to work to love him with all our hearts. The Father often seems to choose those who had been the greatest sinners to pour out his greatest grace, rather than those who walk more innocently. This reveals more of his abundant goodness and grace.

Second Conversation

11

Adore God in Spirit and Truth

To adore God in spirit and in truth is to adore him as we should: God is a spirit; therefore he must be adored in spirit and in truth. What does this really mean? To worship in spirit and truth means that we must worship him with a humble, sincere adoration of spirit in the depth and center of our beings. Only God can see this adoration, which we must repeat so often that at last it becomes natural to us, as if God were one with our soul and our soul were one with God. Practicing this interior adoration will produce this closeness and intimacy between our heavenly Father and ourselves.

Spiritual Maxims

To adore God in truth is to acclaim him for who he is, and ourselves for who we are. To adore God in truth is to recognize truly, actually, and in our heart, that God is who he is—that is to say, infinitely perfect, infinitely adorable, infinitely apart from evil, and so with all the divine attributes. Every man or woman, however little sense he or she may have, would exert all their strength to pay respect and adoration to this great God.

To adore God in truth is to admit, moreover, that we are just the opposite, and that he is willing to make us like him if we allow him to do so. Who would be so rash as to turn aside for even a moment from the respect, the love, the service, and the continual adoration that we owe him?

Spiritual Maxims

Get into the habit, little by little, of adoring God in this way: Beg for his grace and offer him your heart from time to time—during the day, in the midst of your work, at every moment if you can. Do not constrain yourself by rules or special devotions. Simply turn to God in faith, with love and humility.

Fourth Letter

God does not ask much of you: a little remembrance from time to time, a little adoration, sometimes to ask his grace, sometimes to offer him your pain, other times to thank him for the graces he has given you and still gives. During your meals with your family and in your conversations with your friends, sometimes raise your heart to him, for the least little remembrance will always be very pleasing to him. For this purpose, you need not pray very loudly; he is nearer to us than we think.

Fourth Letter

Always consider God and his glory whenever we are doing something or saying something. Let our goal be to become the most perfect adorers of God in this life, just like we hope to be through all eternity. We must make a firm resolution to over-come, with God's grace, all the difficulties we meet as we walk in the spiritual life.

Spiritual Maxims

At our work and other times during the day—even when we read the scriptures and write on spiritual topics, or during our formal vocal prayers—let us stop for a few minutes, as often as we can, to adore God in the depths of our hearts, to enjoy him, as it were, in passing and in secret. Since you are not unaware that God is present before you during your actions, that he is in the depth and center of your heart, why should you not stop your exterior occupations—at least from time to time—and even your vocal prayers, to adore him interiorly, to praise him, petition him, to offer him your heart, and to thank him?

Spiritual Maxims

I do not intend to ask you to leave the external things of this world forever; that is not realistic. The wisdom of the Holy Spirit must guide you. Nevertheless, I believe that it is a common mistake of spiritual persons not to leave their external surroundings from time to time to adore God within themselves and to enjoy in peace some few moments in his divine presence.

Spiritual Maxims